For my children and my mom, thank you for the spontaneous living room dance parties that often helped me remember my magic.
-*Gina Bell*

To all the beautiful souls,
may you find your rainbow and never let go.
-*Elena Mykolaitis*

TEARS & TULLE

Written by **GINA BELL**   Illustrated by **ELENA MYKOLAITIS**

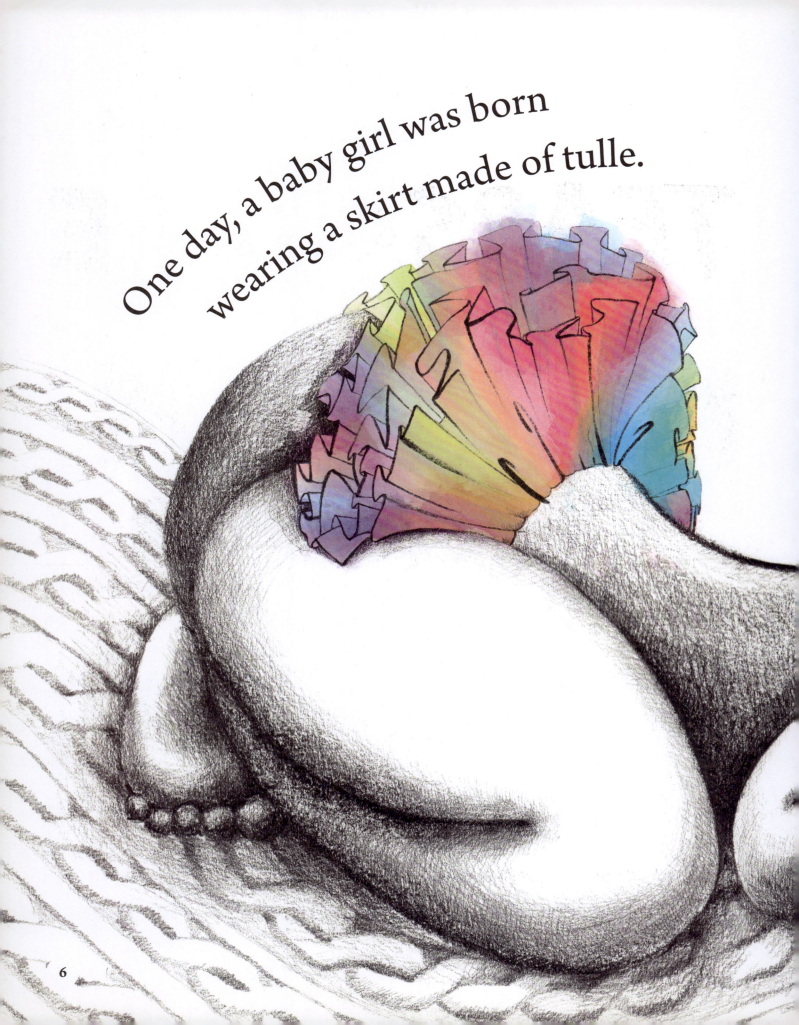

One day, a baby girl was born wearing a skirt made of tulle.

It was bright and colorful, like a **RAINBOW** jewel!

The skirt was invisible, seen just by the girl.

She giggled happily,
watching its wild colors swirl!

The skirt connected the girl to her magic, color, and dreams.

When she was full of tears, the skirt sent her heart joyful beams!

As the girl grew and grew, the magical skirt did too!

Soon, she realized that life could be messy and unfair.

She needed to remember her skirt would always be there!

She fluffed her skirt
and jumped to her feet.

She would wake up the skirt
with her own special beat!

Skip! Dance! Swish! Twirl!

Remember the SPIRIT of that magical girl!

Sometimes she felt scared, embarrassed, and like she didn't have a clue.

So she fluffed her skirt and remembered the fun of trying something new!

There were times she felt left out, misunderstood, and like she would never fit in.

So she fluffed her skirt and remembered to be comfortable in her own skin!

Remember the **SPIRIT** of that magical girl!

And when life was just too much, and her eyes filled with tears,

she fluffed her skirt and remembered she could learn from her fears!

The tears made her wise and watered the dream in her heart.

Fluffing her skirt, she remembered she was a growing work of art!

Remember the SPIRIT of that magical girl!

As she grew older, her days could feel overwhelming, crazy, and long.

So she fluffed her skirt and remembered she was radiant, resilient, and strong!

Sometimes it felt like her life was falling apart at the seams.

So she fluffed her skirt and remembered she could always connect to her dreams!

She celebrated her failures and the lessons they taught her along the way.

She fluffed her skirt and remembered she had something important to say!

She trusted the wisdom in her heart
to help others grow, learn, and heal.

Fluffing her skirt,
she remembered
her struggles made
her beautiful and real!

Skip! Dance! Swish! Twirl!

Remember the SPIRIT of EVERY magical girl!

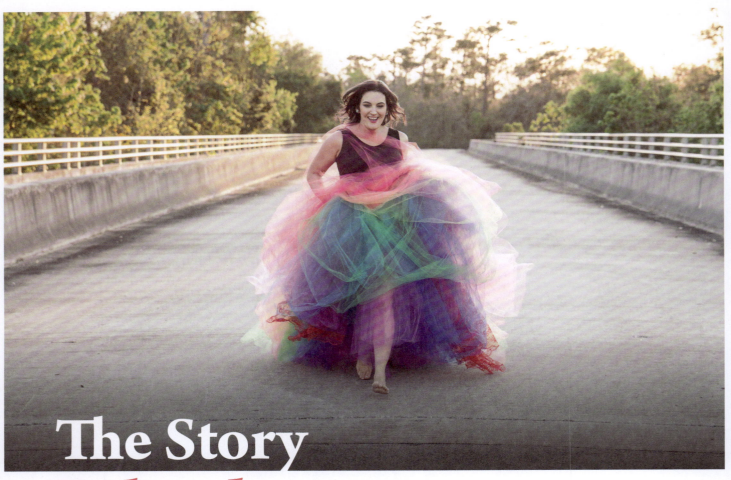

The Story Behind the Skirt

Hi! My name is Gina Bell. I'm the creator of Tears & Tulle, a women's empowerment movement that celebrates women who show up from within the chaos of everyday life to connect with their magic!

In 2018, my life changed on an abandoned overpass in Orlando, Florida. I was wearing a simple black tank and the most magical rainbow-colored tulle skirt. I had purposefully paired the colorful skirt with a black t-shirt to relay a special message to myself and people everywhere. We don't need to wait for life's perfect set of circumstances to connect with our extraordinary color.

My purpose with the Tears and Tulle movement

is to reconnect women with their joy and color, even during life's darkest moments. It may sound strange, but the rainbow skirt woke up something wonderful in me! I want women everywhere to experience what I did, a clarifying moment of vulnerability, magic, and happiness.

A year and a half after that day on the overpass, I launched Tears & Tulle. I'm sharing the rainbow skirt with fifty-two people over fifty-two weeks as a way to inspire women everywhere to reconnect with their color (tulle) from within the darkness (tears) of real life.

The Story Behind the Skirt

While organizing the movement, I learned that my friend and rainbow tulle skirt designer, Cassandra Youngs, had always hoped that one of her creations would travel the world. She loved that our two ideas would become one!

Each woman in the movement is asked to pair the skirt with something black, make their unique magic in it, and share their Tears & Tulle story with the world. Time after time, participants have shared how much love and positive energy the rainbow skirt radiates. Many participants used their time with the skirt to reflect on their greatest struggles. That's what Tears & Tulle is all about. Embracing our perfectly imperfect lives.

The Tears & Tulle movement continues to grow and evolve in amazing ways. You can join the movement by starting a T&T tribe or becoming a T&T trailblazer! Learn more at www.ginabell.co.

The Story Behind the Skirt

— Black Bark Books —

WITH THANKS TO EVERYONE WHO SUPPORTED THIS DREAM FROM THE VERY BEGINNING.

WITH SPECIAL THANKS TO MY CHILDREN, ROB, DAD, TOTO, AND AUNT STACEY.

CREDITS:
Written by: Gina Bell
Illustrated by: Elena Mykolaitis
Designed by: Paul Ranalli
Edited by: Saskia Lacey and Samantha Marino

Library of Congress Control Number: 2020918374
ISBN: 978-1-7353867-0-6

©2020 by Gina Bell LLC. All rights reserved. No part of this book may be reproduced in any form or by any electronic or mechanical means, including information storage and retrieval systems, not known or to be invented without written permission in writing from the author, except by reviewers, who may quote brief passages in a review. Contact: gina@thetearsandtullemovement.com or www.ginabell.co Tears & Tulle is a trademark of Gina Bell LLC.

Participant/Photographer Credits:

https://www.ginabell.co/wheres-the-skirt

1st Printing by Puffer Print - Puffer Print is a Climate Neutral Certified company

Printed in China with soy inks.